GEORGE WINSTON
PIANO SHEET MUSIC COLLECTION

Exact Transcriptions From The Recordings
Authorized by **GEORGE WINSTON**

ISBN 978-1-5400-5604-7

Visit Hal Leonard Online at
www.halleonard.com

Contact us:
Hal Leonard
7777 West Bluemound Road
Milwaukee, WI 53213
Email: info@halleonard.com

In Europe, contact:
Hal Leonard Europe Limited
42 Wigmore Street
Marylebone, London, W1U 2RN
Email: info@halleonardeurope.com

In Australia, contact:
Hal Leonard Australia Pty. Ltd.
4 Lentara Court
Cheltenham, Victoria, 3192 Australia
Email: info@halleonard.com.au

NOTES FROM GEORGE WINSTON

These are exact transcriptions of 12 songs from my albums, with chords included. One should feel free to interpret and change them however they want—I do that with all the songs that I play. (These transcribed versions are just the way the songs were played on the days that I recorded them.) I learn music by ear, and I use chords and music theory to learn and remember music. (See next page.)

One of the reasons I play the piano is that I prefer the quality of the sustain that the piano has, more than strings or organ, etc. I often use the sustain pedal for extended time periods, so sometimes some of the notes will sound like they are struck, but what is actually happening is that when the pedal is held down for a while, the overtones will sometimes swell and sound like a softly struck note. In this book these types of sustained notes are indicated with a tie. You could strike those notes if you prefer.

The other reason I play the piano is because of its power and volume, and because it is possible to play a lot of songs with multiple parts as solo instrumentals, which is my temperament as a musician. I often think of the piano as if it is an Afro-American tuned drum.

Many thanks to Tom Bockhold for doing the initial transcriptions that I later fine-tuned while listening to the recordings, and for being so great to work with, and for understanding so well my unusual ways of playing and working. Also thanks to Kathleen A. Harrill, BS, MT-BC for her wonderful assistance.

Whether you learn music by ear or from the written page, I suggest learning chords (any combination of three notes or more played together), and music theory (how chords are used in the different music traditions).

Any piece of written music can be analyzed in terms of its chord structure. The individual notes are like the letters in the alphabet, and chords are like words. The **Major** and **minor** chords are the building blocks for all other chords. Becoming familiar with chord structures can aid in memorization.

Suggested order for learning chords:

1. **Major** chords, which have the 1st, 3rd, and 5th notes of the Major scale of a key.
2. **minor** chords, which have the 3rd lowered a half step (down one note).
3. **Dominant** 7th chords, the **minor** 7th chords, and the **Major** 7th chords.
4. **Ninth** chords (adding the 9th note with those three types of 7th chords mentioned just above in #3).
5. **diminished** chords (and the diminished 7th chords), and the augmented chords.
6. **Major** 6th and the **minor** 6th chords.
7. Then you may want to learn the jazz chords – **13th** chords, **flat 9th** chords, augmented 9th chords, **flat 5** chords (sometimes called **augmented 11th** chords), **11th** chords, and more.
8. and then you could study scales and modes that are associated with the different chords (if you know the chords, then you already know 3, 4, or 5 of the notes of the seven note associated scale).

Again, any combination of three notes or more can be called a chord (and actually any chord could be interpreted in twelve different ways, interpreting the chord in the twelve keys).

CHORD STRUCTURE

Key	Major	Minor
C	C-E-G	C-Eb-G
D flat (aka C#)	Db-F-Ab (aka C#-F-G#)	Db-E-Ab (aka C#-E-G#)
D	D-F#-A	D-F-A
E flat	Eb-G-Bb	Eb-Gb-Bb
E	E-G#-B	E-G-B
F	F-A-C	F-Ab-C
G flat (aka F#)	Gb-Bb-Db (aka F#-Bb-C#)	Gb-A-Db (aka F#-A-C#)
G	G-B-D	G-Bb-D
A flat	Ab-C-Eb	Ab-B-Eb
A	A-C#-E	A-C-E
B flat	Bb-D-F	Bb-Db-F
B	B-D#-F#	B-D-F#

PRACTICE PRIORITIES

When working out the chord and/or techniques, licks, etc. to practice on the piano, these are the suggested priority order of keys (Major and minor):

1	C, F, G, Eb, & Bb	by far the most commonly used keys in the R&B and Jazz traditions; and 99% of Boogie-Woogie piano songs are in the keys of C, F, G
2	Ab	sometimes used in the R&B and Jazz traditions
3	A	commonly used key in Blues when playing with guitarists
4	E & D	also commonly used keys in the Blues when playing with guitarists
5	Db (C#) & Gb (F#)	rarely used
6	B	the key of B Major is the most rarely used key; B minor is used a bit more

A great book for exploring more about chords is Picture Chord Encyclopedia for Keyboard (HL.310978). This book has photos, diagrams, and music notation for over 1,600 keyboard chords. See www.halleonard.com.

For more information about how George plays the piano, guitar, and/or harmonica, go to www.georgewinston.com, click on "ABOUT", then "Q & A", then select the appropriate section: "Piano Related Questions", "Guitar Related Questions" or "Harmonica Related Questions".

To see the Complete Workshop Document (with information on chords, ear training, modes, solo guitar, solo harmonic, and more) go to www.georgewinston.com, then to "ABOUT," then "Q &A," then "Piano Related Questions," then "Question #4" Do You Give Workshsops? What materials do you make available at workshops? Various workshop documents are here to download.

SONG NOTES

Bird of Prey - from my solo piano album, NIGHT DIVIDES THE DAY – THE MUSIC OF THE DOORS. Originally sung a cappella by Jim Morrison, during his March 1969 poetry reading studio session (one of two poetry sessions he did, the other one on December 8, 1970). This song was first issued in 1995, as a bonus track on the CD version of his posthumous poetry album AN AMERICAN PRAYER, originally issued in 1978.

Cold Cloudy Morning (Carousel 2 in G minor) – from my solo piano album, SPRING CAROUSEL – A CANCER RESEARCH BENEFIT

Early Morning Range – from my solo piano album, SUMMER. Inspired by mornings in eastern Montana.

Elcina's Grandmother's Rag – A bonus track from my solo piano album, BALLADS AND BLUES 1972. Inspired by Leila Kyte McMillian (1888-1981), and her daughter Ina Mason, and her granddaughter Gwen Elcina Fiske, and people and places around Canandaigua, New York.

Frangenti - from my solo piano album, PLAINS. A love song by the Italian mandolinist and composer, Massimo Gatti. My arrangement was inspired by the version by Butch Baldassari, (1952-2009), on his album with the Nashville Mandolin Ensemble, PLECTRASONICS.

January Stars - from my solo piano album, WINTER INTO SPRING Inspired by winter nights in Billings, Montana.

Japanese Music Box (Itsuki No Komoriuta) - from my solo piano album, FOREST. A traditional Japanese lullaby. The title means Lullaby of Itsuki, a region in southern Japan near the city of Kumumoto.

Love Song to a Ballerina - from my solo piano album, FOREST. By composer Mark Isham from the children's story soundtrack THE STEADFAST TIN SOLDIER. Other great children's story soundtracks by Mark Isham include THUMBELINA and THE EMPEROR AND THE NIGHTINGALE (all three were produced by Rabbit Ears Productions www.rabbitears.com.) I also recorded his composition *Thumbelina* on my album MONTANA-A LOVE STORY.

More Than You Know - from my solo piano album, SPRING CAROUSEL – A CANCER RESEARCH BENEFIT.

Music Box (Kojo No Tsuki) - from my solo piano album, MONTANA – A LOVE STORY. A piece composed in 1901, by the renowned Japanese composer, Rentaro Taki (1879-1903), for a poem written by the Sendai poet, Bansui Doi. They were inspired by the ruins of the Okajyo Castle, built in 1185, and located in Taketa City, Oita Prefecture, in southern Japan. The title can be translated as "The Moon Over the Old Castle."

Room at the Bottom – from my solo piano album, LOVE WILL COME – THE MUSIC OF VINCE GUARALDI VOLUME 2. I have always related music to seasons and places, and here I play this piece evocative of the San Francisco nights. Vince Guaraldi recorded it on his album JAZZ IMPRESSIONS, with tracks from 1957, and on his album A FLOWER IS A LOVESOME THING, with tracks also from 1957, and the song was titled *Like a Mighty Rose* on that album (the same track is on both albums).

Waltz for the Lonely – from my solo piano album, PLAINS. This beautiful ballad by the great guitarist, Chet Atkins (1924-2001), worked best for me as a piano solo. Chet recorded it on his video, CHET ATKINS AND FRIENDS - MUSIC FROM THE HEART, and on his recording, THE MAGIC OF CHET ATKINS (Heartland Records).

DISCOGRAPHY

SOLO PIANO ALBUMS

1. **BALLADS AND BLUES 1972** (1972)
2. **AUTUMN** (1980)
3. **DECEMBER** (1982)
4. **WINTER INTO SPRING** (1982)
5. **SUMMER** (1991)
6. **FOREST** (1994)
7. **LINUS & LUCY – THE MUSIC OF VINCE GUARALDI Vol. 1** (1996)
8. **PLAINS** (1999)
9. **NIGHT DIVIDES THE DAY - THE MUSIC OF THE DOORS** (2002)
10. **MONTANA – A LOVE STORY** (2004)
11. **GULF COAST BLUES & IMPRESSIONS Vol. 1 – A HURRICANE RELIEF BENEFIT** (2006)
12. **LOVE WILL COME – THE MUSIC OF VINCE GUARALDI Vol. 2** (2010)
13. **GULF COAST BLUES & IMPRESSIONS Vol. 2 – A LOUISIANA WETLANDS BENEFIT** (2012)
14. **SPRING CAROUSEL – A CANCER RESEARCH BENEFIT** (2017)
15. **RESTLESS WIND** (2019)

OTHER RECORDINGS

1. **THE VELVETEEN RABBIT** (1984) Solo piano soundtrack with narration by Meryl Streep
2. **SADAKO AND THE THOUSAND PAPER CRANES** (1995) Solo guitar soundtrack with narration by Liv Ullmann
3. **REMEMBRANCE – A MEMORIAL BENEFIT** (2001) EP, includes piano, guitar, and harmonica solos
4. **HARMONICA SOLOS** (2012) Solo harmonica pieces
5. **SILENT NIGHT – BENEFIT SINGLE FOR FEEDING AMERICA** (2013) Solo piano

BIRD OF PREY

from the solo piano album NIGHT DIVIDES THE DAY - THE MUSIC OF THE DOORS

Words and Music by JOHN DENSMORE,
ROBBY KRIEGER, RAY MANZAREK
and JIM MORRISON
Arranged by George Winston

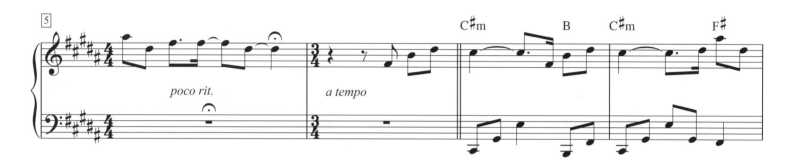

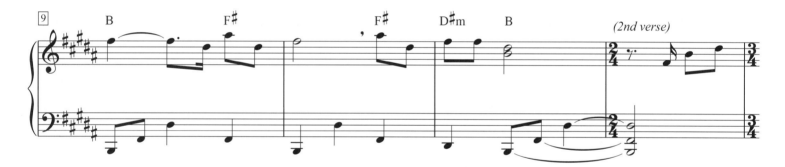

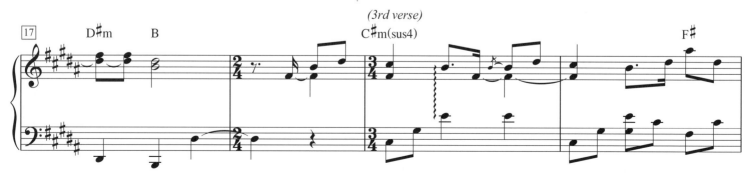

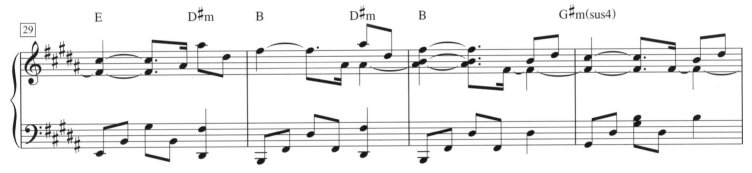

COLD CLOUDY MORNING
(Carousel 2 in G minor)
from the solo piano album SPRING CAROUSEL - A CANCER RESEARCH BENEFIT

By GEORGE WINSTON

EARLY MORNING RANGE

from the solo piano album SUMMER

By GEORGE WINSTON

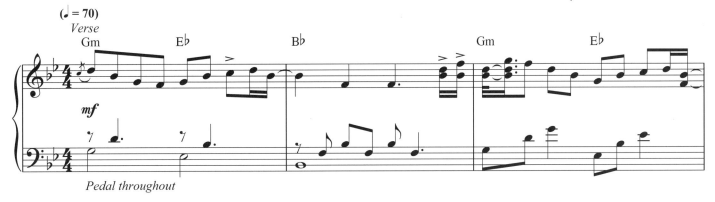

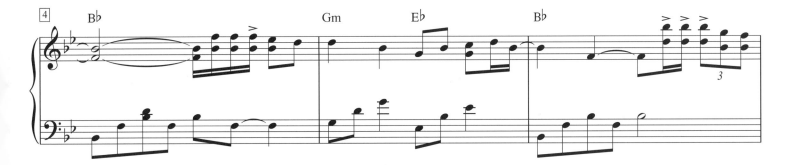

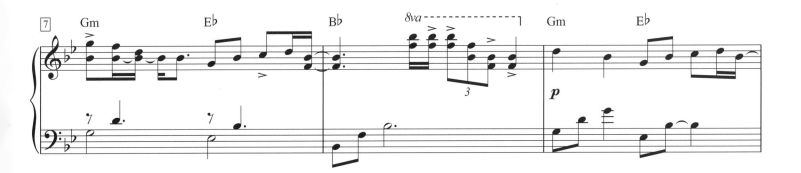

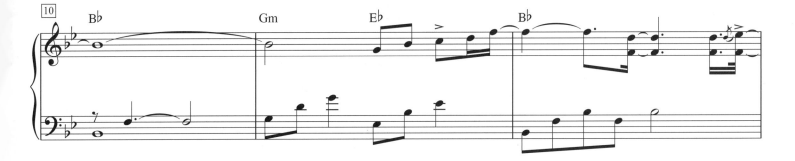

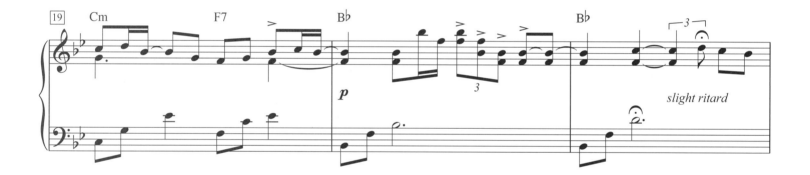

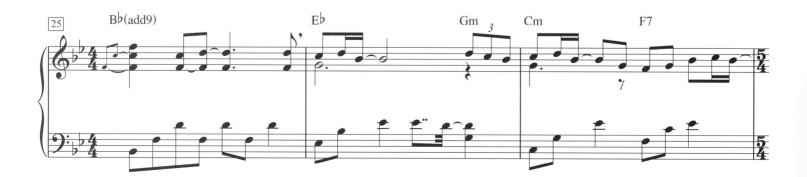

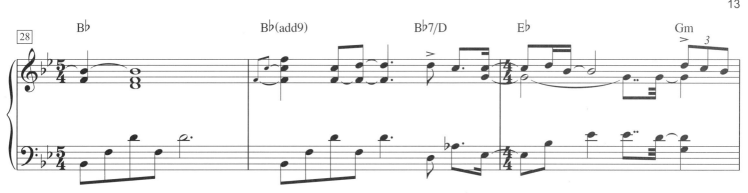

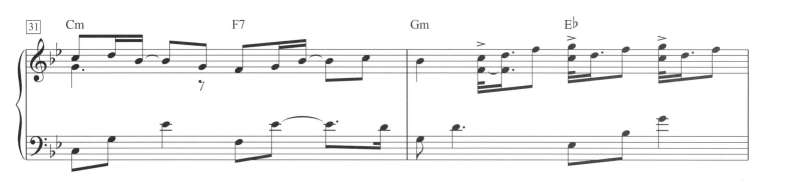

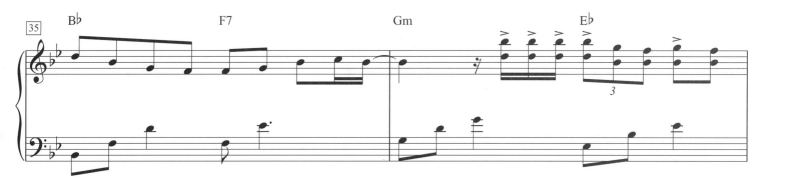

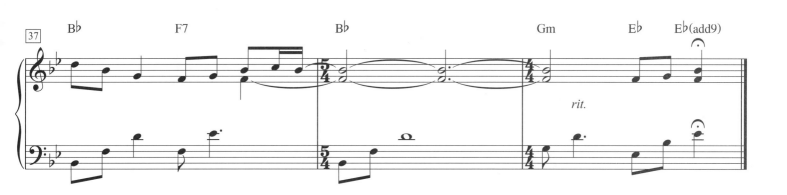

ELCINA'S GRANDMOTHER'S RAG

bonus track from the solo piano album BALLADS AND BLUES 1972

By GEORGE WINSTON

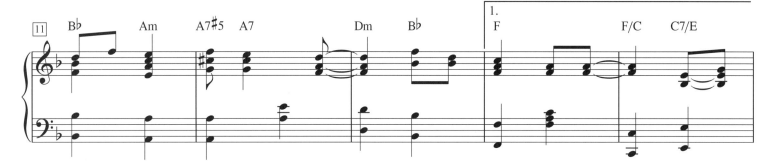

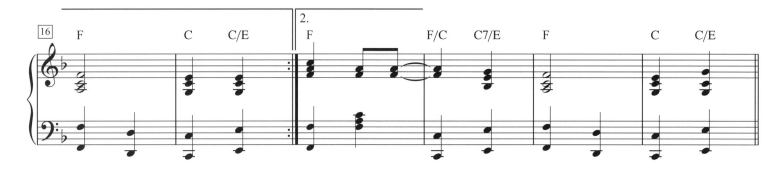

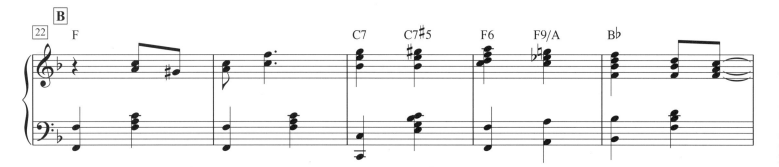

15

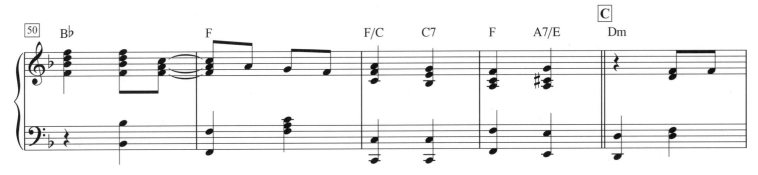

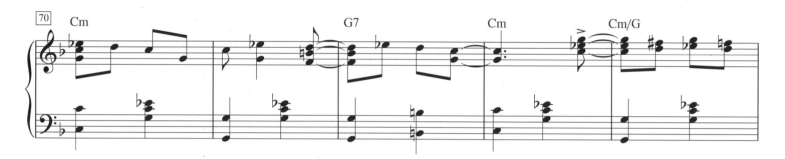

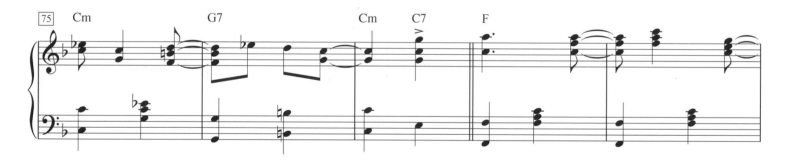

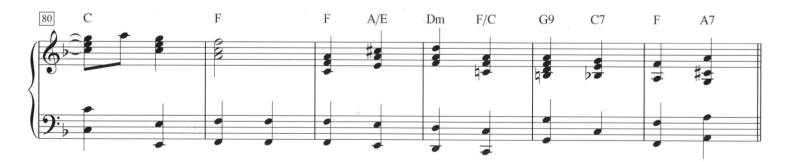

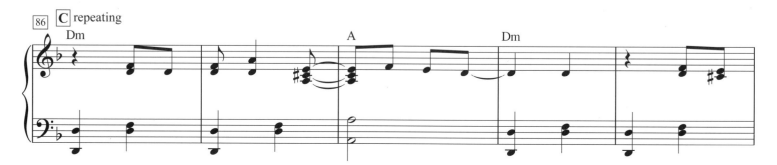

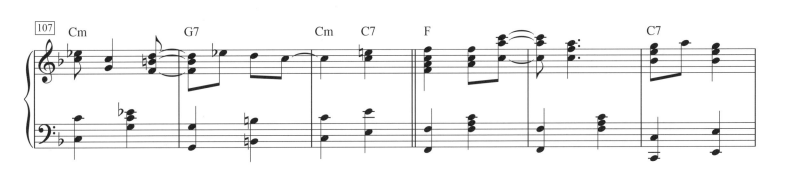

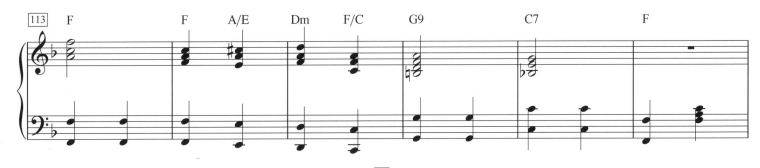

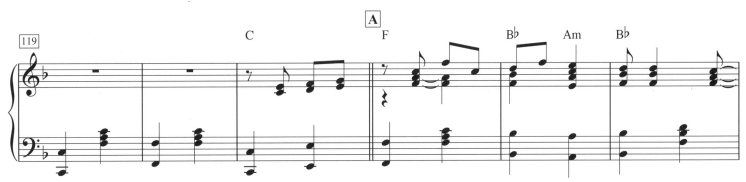

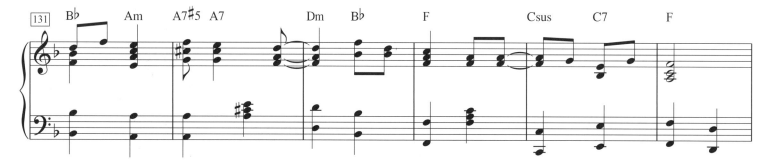

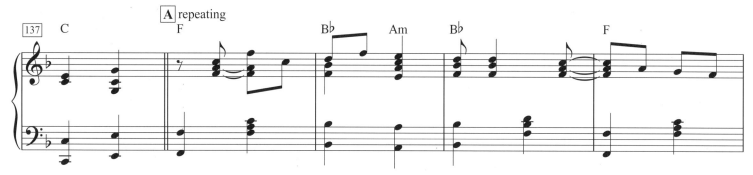

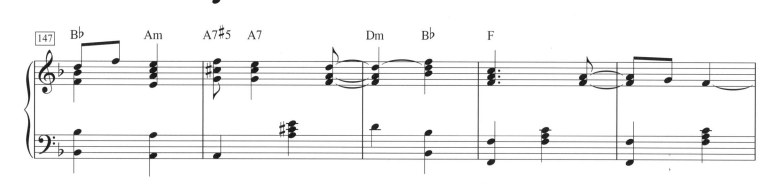

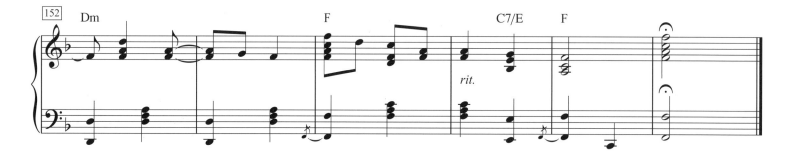

FRANGENTI
from the solo piano album PLAINS

Words and Music by
MASSIMO GATTI
Arranged by George Winston

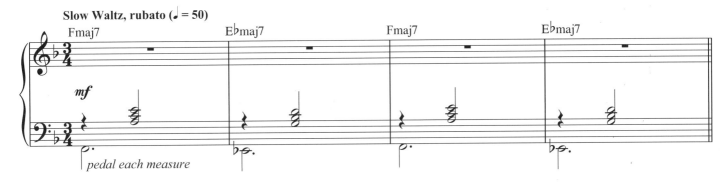

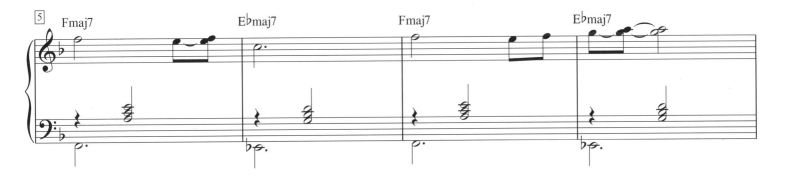

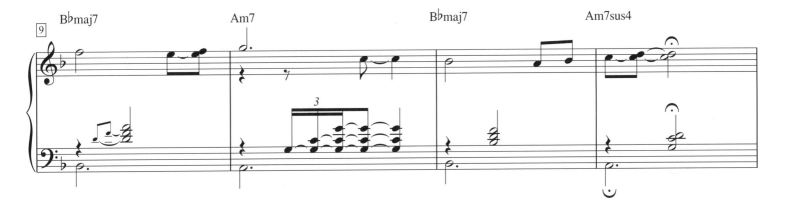

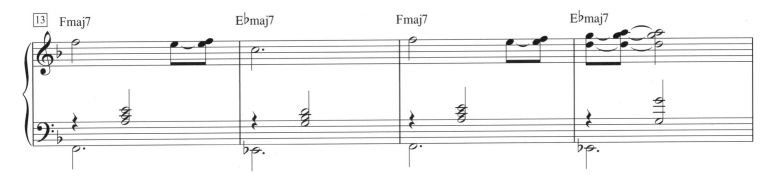

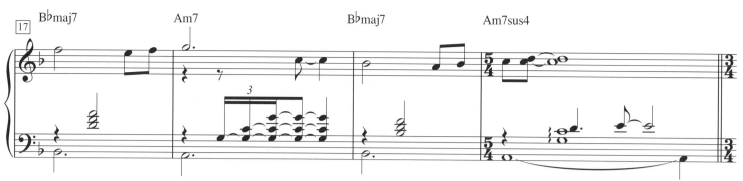

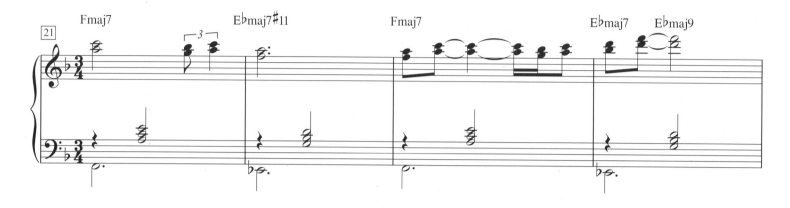

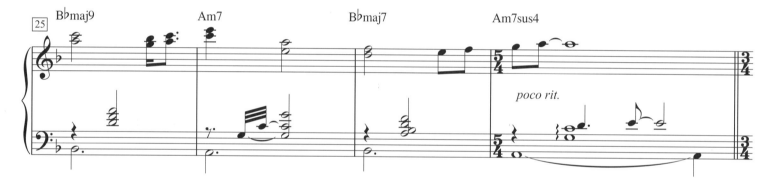

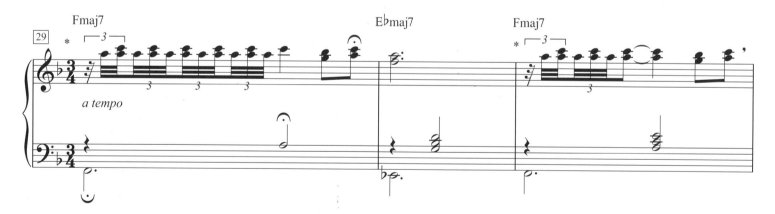

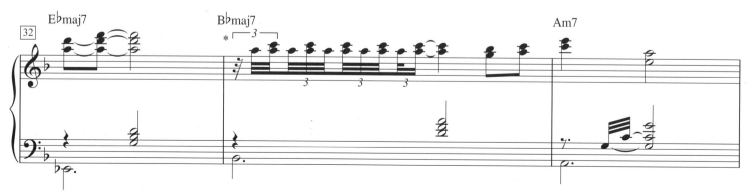

This applies to measures 29, 31 & 33 - I use rapid repeats on the lower note with the middle finger and the thumb, with the little finger playing the higher note half the amount of time of the lower note - this is to get a mandolin-type sound.

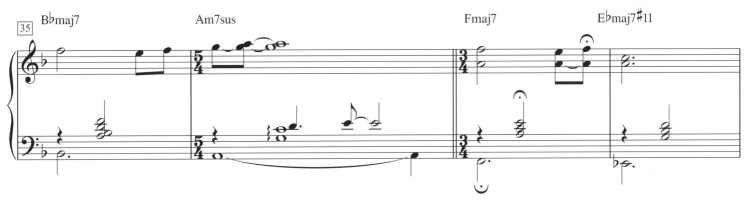

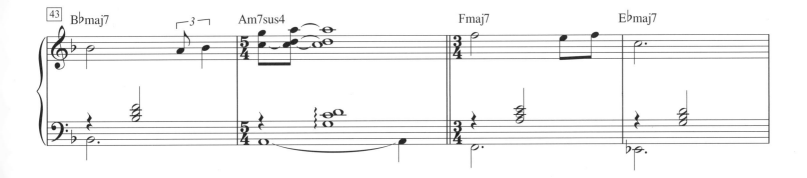

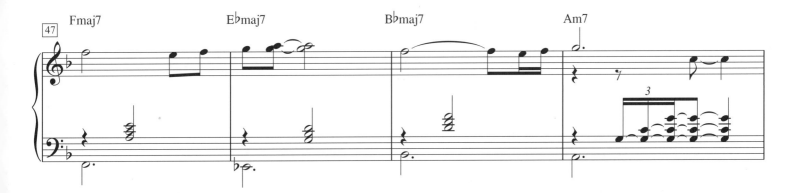

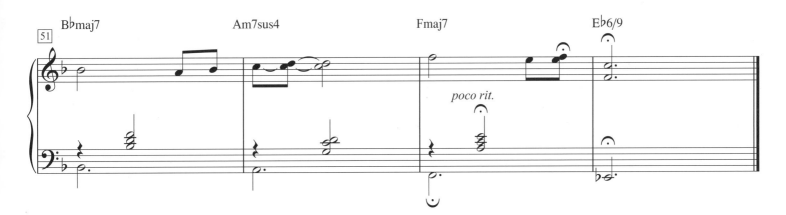

JANUARY STARS
from the solo piano album WINTER INTO SPRING

By GEORGE WINSTON

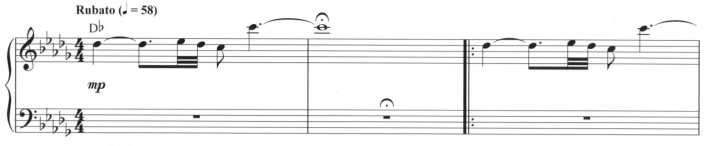

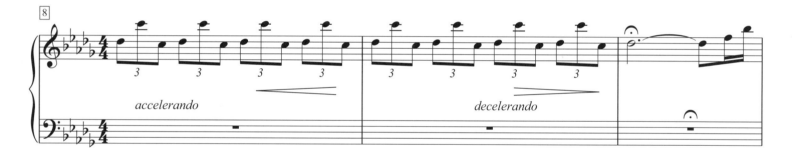

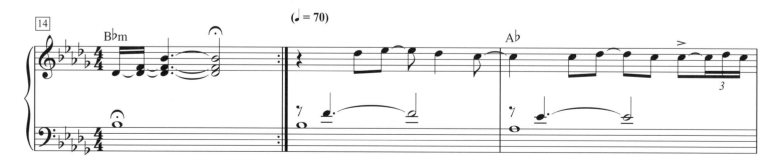

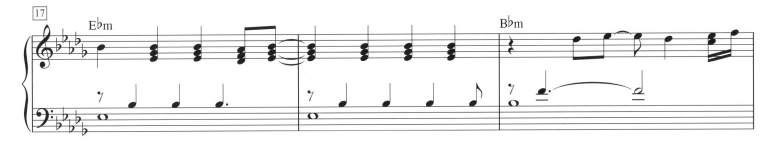

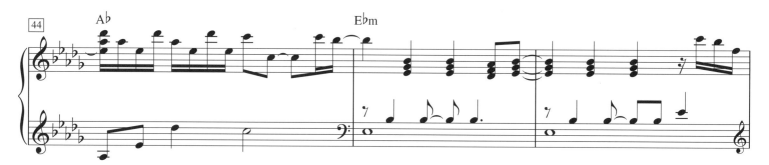

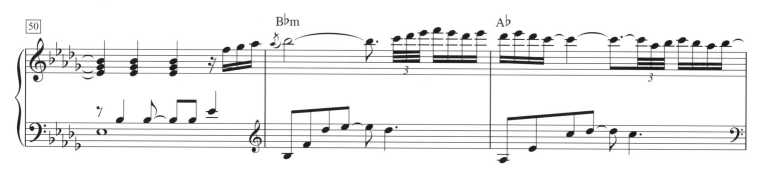

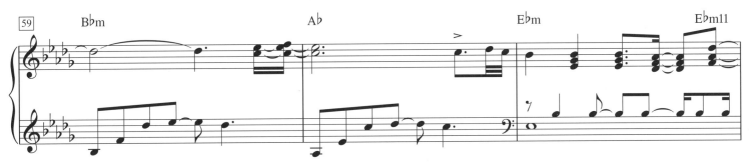

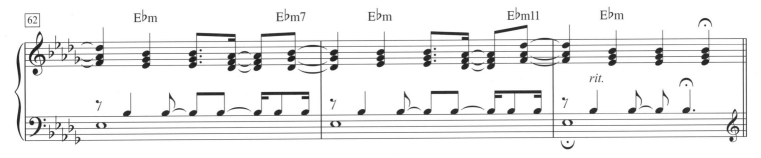

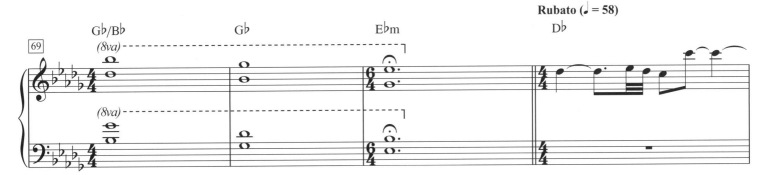

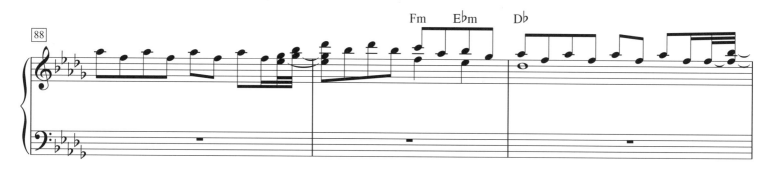

MORE THAN YOU KNOW

from the solo piano album SPRING CAROUSEL - A CANCER RESEARCH BENEFIT

By GEORGE WINSTON

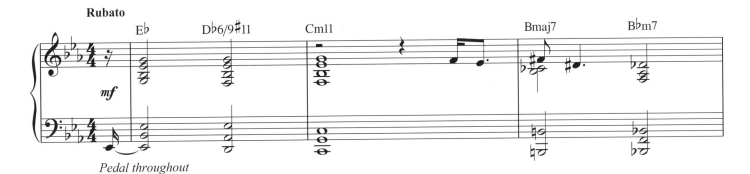

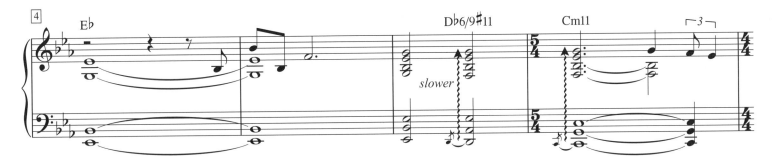

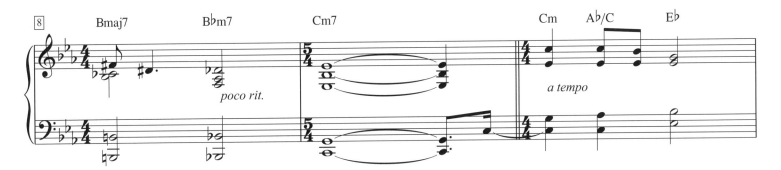

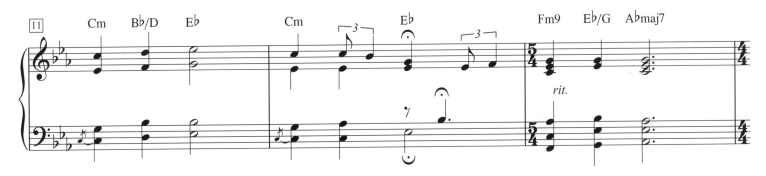

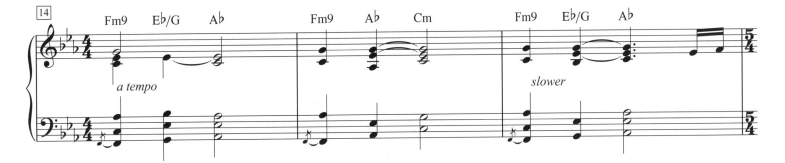

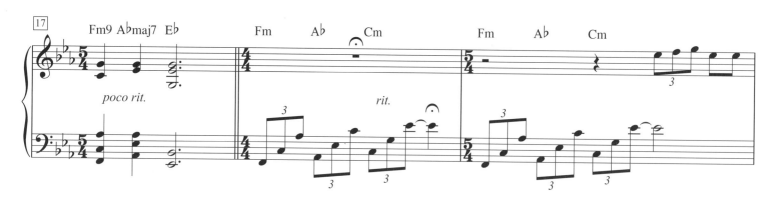

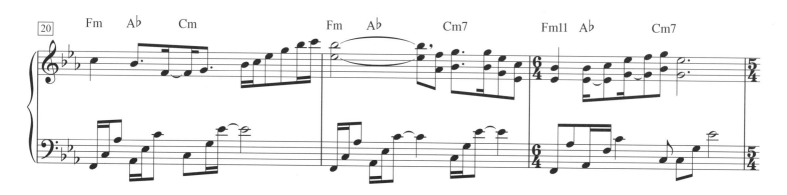

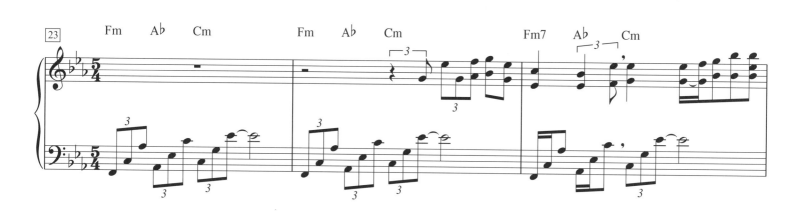

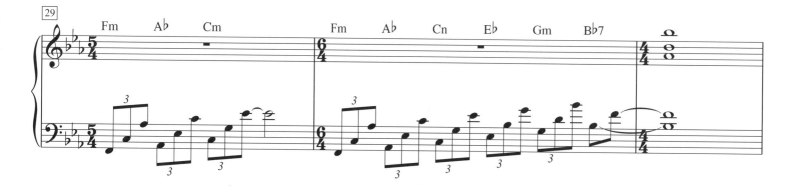

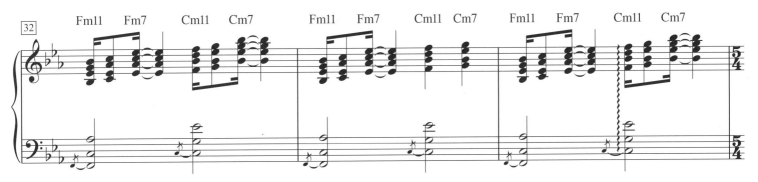

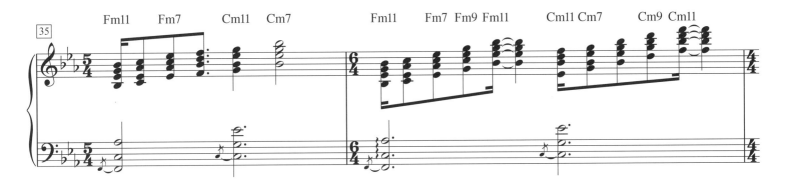

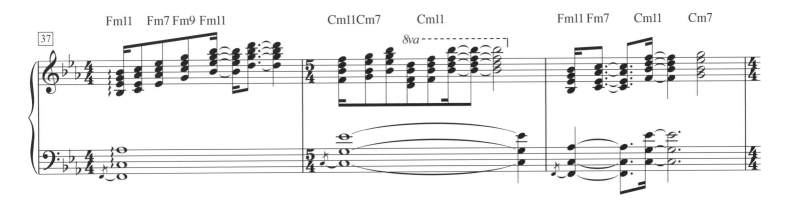

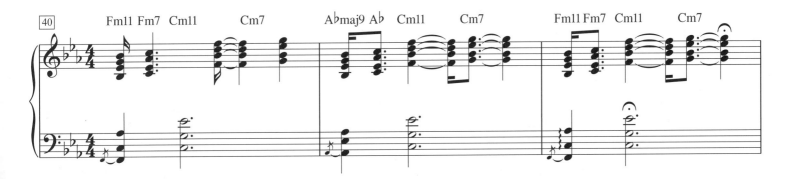

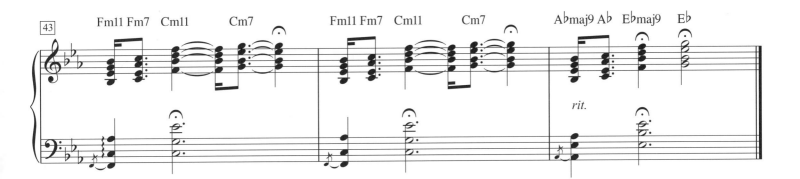

JAPANESE MUSIC BOX
(Itsuki No Komoriuta)
from the solo piano album FOREST

Traditional Japanese Lullaby
Arranged by George Winston

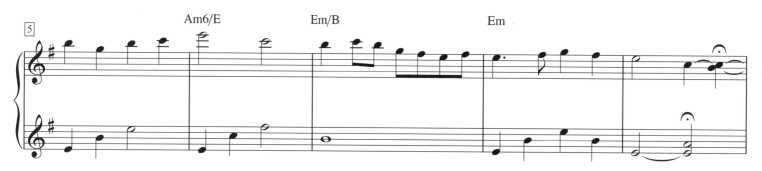

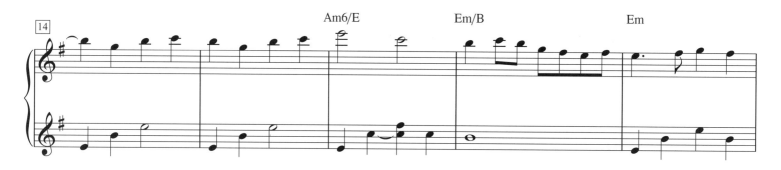

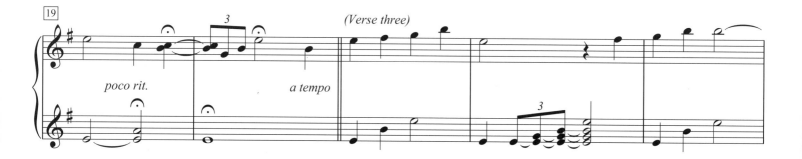

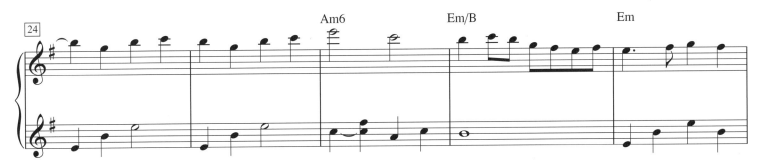

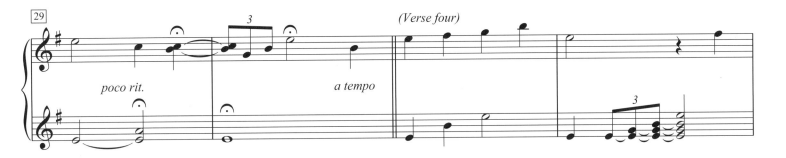

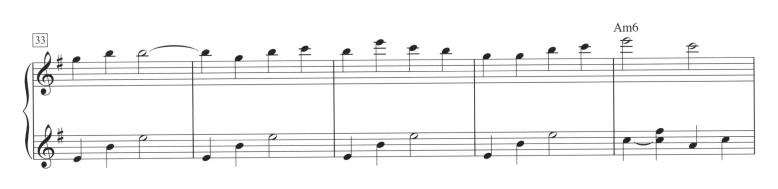

LOVE SONG TO A BALLERINA

from the solo piano album FOREST

Music by MARK ISHAM
Arranged by George Winston

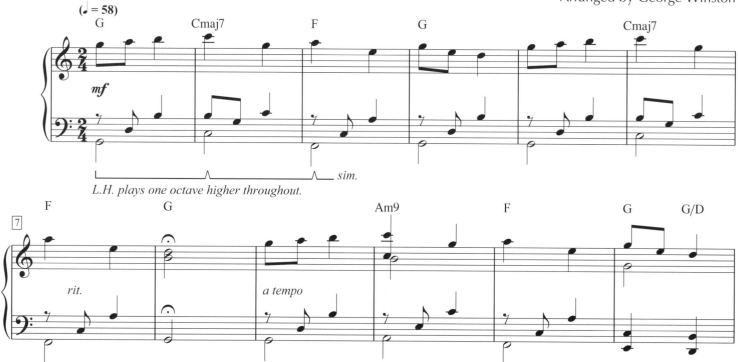

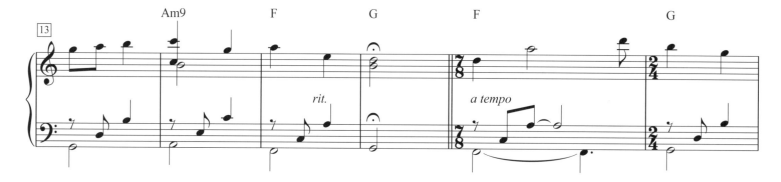

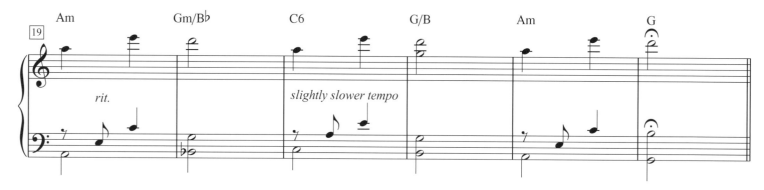

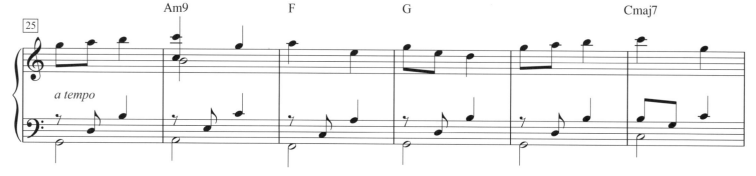

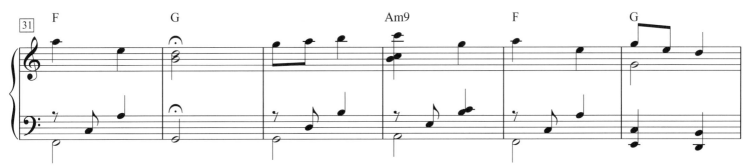

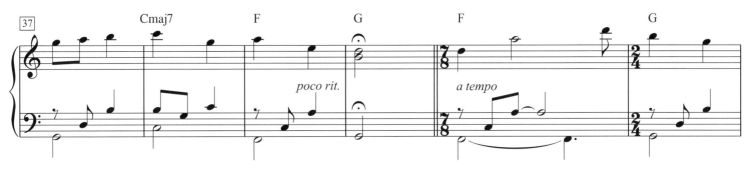

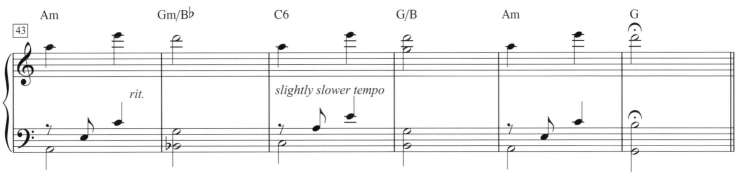

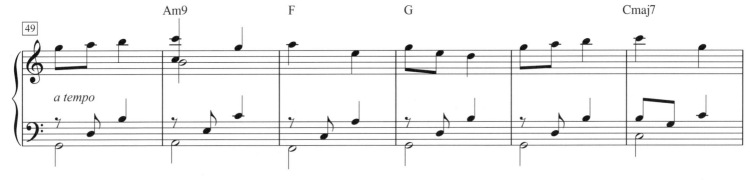

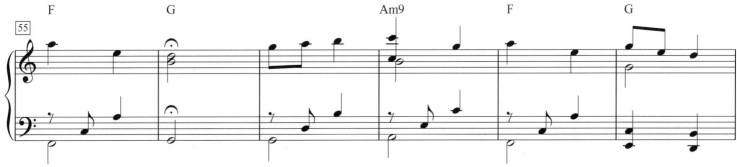

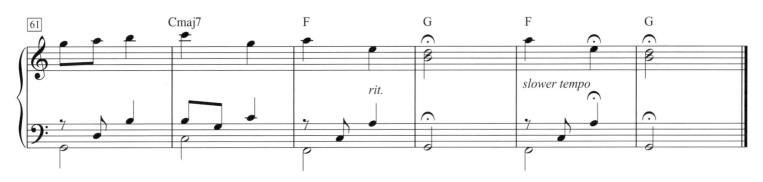

MUSIC BOX
(Kojo No Tsuki)
from the solo piano album MONTANA - A LOVE STORY

Music by RENTARY TAKI
Arranged by George Winston

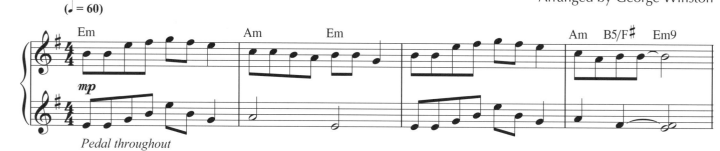

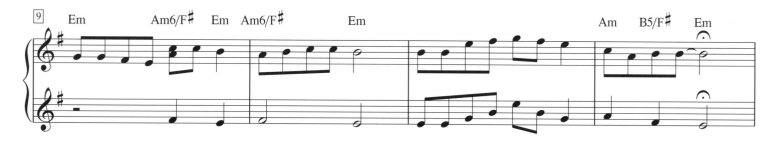

WALTZ FOR THE LONELY

from the solo piano album PLAINS

Words and Music by CHET ATKINS
and RANDY GOODRUM
Arranged by George Winston

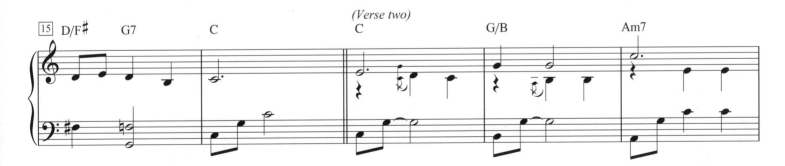

*In measures 49–58 I personally play the rapid repeated notes with thumb and 3rd finger.

ROOM AT THE BOTTOM
from the solo piano album LOVE WILL COME - THE MUSIC OF VINCE GUARALDI

By VINCE GUARALDI
Arranged by George Winston

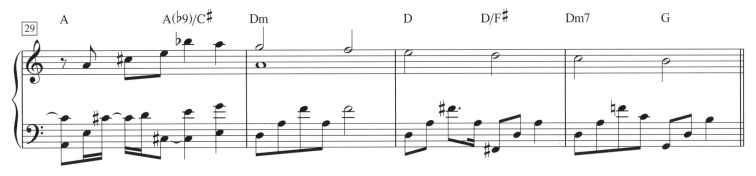

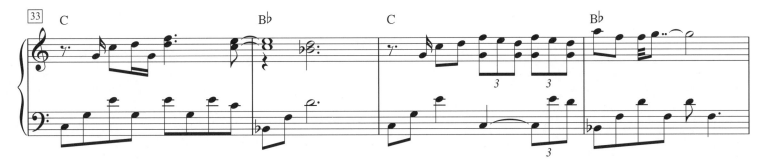

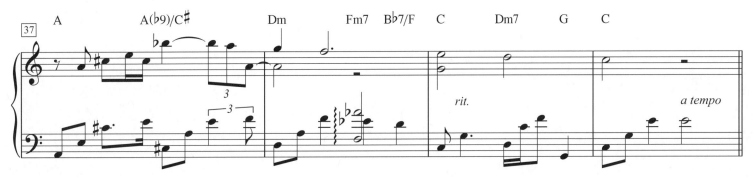

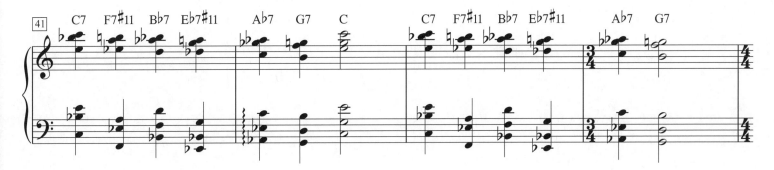

George Winston grew up mainly in Montana, and spent his later formative years in Mississippi and Florida. During this time, his favorite music was instrumental rock and instrumental R&B, including Floyd Cramer, the Ventures, Booker T & The MG's, Jimmy Smith, and many more. Inspired by R&B, jazz, Blues and rock (especially the Doors), George began playing organ in 1967. In 1971 he switched to the acoustic piano after hearing recordings from the 1920s and the 1930s by the legendary stride pianists Thomas "Fats" Waller and the late Teddy Wilson. In addition to working on stride piano, he also came up with his own style of melodic instrumental music on solo piano, called folk piano.

Since 1972, George has released fifteen solo piano albums. His most recent albums are RESTLESS WIND and SPRING CAROUSEL- A CANCER RESEARCH BENEFIT. He also recorded the soundtracks for three video projects produced by the late George Levenson of Informed Democracy (**www.informeddemocracy.com**): a solo guitar soundtrack for SADAKO AND THE THOUSAND PAPER CRANES, as well as piano, guitar, and harmonica solos for PUMPKIN CIRCLE and BREAD COMES TO LIFE. In addition, he recorded the solo piano soundtrack for the Rabbit Ears video of the children's story, THE VELVETEEN RABBIT (www.rabbitears.com), and the soundtrack for the Peanuts episode, THIS IS AMERICA CHARLIE BROWN: THE BIRTH OF THE CONSTITUTION.

George is presently concentrating mainly on live performances, and most of the time he is touring, playing solo piano concerts, (the *Summer Show* or the *Winter Show*), solo guitar concerts, solo harmonica concerts, and solo piano dances (with R&B and slow dance songs).

He is currently most inspired by the great New Orleans R&B pianists Henry Butler, James Booker, Professor Longhair, Dr. John, and Jon Cleary; and he is also working on interpreting pieces on solo piano by many of his favorite composers, especially Vince Guaraldi, Professor Longhair, and the Doors, as well as Dr. John, Allen Toussaint, Ralph Towner, Sam Cooke, Randy Newman, Frank Zappa, Al Kooper, Rahsaan Roland Kirk, John Hartford, Oliver Schroer, Philip Aaberg and others, to play at concerts, and at his solo piano dances.

George is also working on solo guitar, and is recording the masters of the Hawaiian Slack Key guitar for an extensive series of albums for Dancing Cat Records (**www.dancingcat.com**). Slack Key is the name for the beautiful solo fingerstyle guitar tradition, unique to Hawaii, which began in the early 1800s and predated the steel guitar by over half a century.

He is also recording his main inspirations for his harmonica playing—Sam Hinton, Rick Epping, and Curt Bouterse.

Piano: George Winston plays Steinway Pianos
Guitar: Martin D-35 (1966), with low 7th string added
Harmonica: combining Hohner Big Rivers with key of Low D Cross Harp reed plates